ANDREW JACKSON

ENCYCLOPEDIA of PRESIDENTS

Andrew Jackson

Seventh President of the United States

By Alice Osinski

Consultant: Charles Abele, Ph.D.
Social Studies Instructor
Chicago Public School System

CHILDRENS PRESS ®

CHICAGO

The Hermitage, Andrew Jackson's family home near Nashville, Tennessee

Thank you, Mom and Dad

Library of Congress Cataloging-in-Publication Data

Osinski, Alice.
  Andrew Jackson.

  (Encyclopedia of presidents)
  Includes index.
  Summary: Traces the life of the rowdy "Hero of
New Orleans" from his backwoods beginnings through
his military career to his term as seventh president
of the United States.
  1. Jackson, Andrew, 1767-1845—Juvenile literature.
2. Presidents—United States—Biography—Juvenile
literature. 3. United States—Politics and government—
1829-1837—Juvenile literature. [1. Jackson, Andrew,
1767-1845. 2. Presidents] I. Title.
E382.074 1987   973.5'6'0924 [B] [92]   86-29983
ISBN 0-516-01387-4

Childrens Press, Chicago
Copyright ©1987 by Regensteiner Publishing Enterprises, Inc.
All rights reserved. Published simultaneously in Canada.
Printed in the United States of America.
1 2 3 4 5 6 7 8 9 10 R 96 95 94 93 92 91 90 89 88 87

Picture Acknowledgments

The Bettmann Archive—31, 34, 37 (top), 43
(left), 57, 63, 67, 75 (bottom), 84 (top)

Culver Pictures—66

Historical Pictures Service—6, 9, 11, 14, 18, 21
(bottom right), 25, 48, 49, 52, 53, 64, 74, 75
(top), 76, 80, 81, 83, 85 (top), 89

The Ladies' Hermitage Association—20 (bottom
left and right), 29, 36 (top)

Library of Congress—5, 8, 10, 12, 15, 17, 27,
28, 36 (bottom), 38, 40, 41, 43, 44, 46, 47, 56,
58, 60 (bottom left), 86

National Gallery of Art—21 (top)

Nawrocki Stock Photo—20 (top), 21 (bottom
left), 60 (top right), 65, 71, 84 (bottom)

The Newberry Library—45, 55

North Wind Picture Archives—16, 35, 50, 62,
69, 70

Oklahoma Historical Society—54

H. Armstrong Roberts—22, 33, 42, 60 (top left),
78, 79, 85 (bottom)

Root Resources/Mary A. Root—4, 37 (bottom)

U.S. Bureau of Printing and Engraving—2

Western History Collections, University of
Oklahoma Library—68

Woolaroc Museum—72

Cover design and illustration by
Steven Gaston Dobson

Andrew Jackson at the Battle of New Orleans

Table of Contents

B. WEST CLINEDINST. 1896

Chapter 1

Frontier President

By the thousands they came, flooding the unpaved streets to the Capitol building in Washington—country folk and soldiers, laborers and farmers, black and white, rich and poor. They came from the farms and backwoods of America, some from hundreds of miles away. All hoped to catch a glimpse of the man who symbolized the beginning of a new era in America. Pressing nearer to the Capitol steps, the crowd waited to hear the words of the man who had become the voice of the common people.

On that late winter afternoon in 1829, the roar of the crowd seemed to "shake the very ground." Nearly fifteen thousand people cheered as the thin, six-foot-one, sixty-one-year-old man appeared on the inauguration platform. Major General Andrew Jackson raised his steel-blue eyes and softly repeated the oath of office to become the seventh president of the United States. Slowly he turned his pale face, pockmarked from smallpox and deeply scarred from battle wounds, to the impatient crowd. "I will not fail you," he said. The crowd let out another chilling cry, muffling the rest of Jackson's ten-minute speech.

Opposite page: Jackson's inauguration day

GEN ANDREW JACKSON

Was born at Waxsaw, South Carolina March 15th 1767, two years after his father emigrated from Ireland, at 14 years of age he entered the army of the revolution, and was wounded and captured, escaping from the enemy he commenced the study of law, and was admitted to practice in 1788, elected member of Congress from Tennessee in 1796, and in 1797 elected member of the National Senate, but resigned at the end of the first session, upon which he was appointed Judge of the supreme court of Tennessee which appointment he soon after resigned, he was also appointed Major Gen of the Tennessee Militia in 1776, in 1812 he was ordered to take the field against the Indians in the south, and in all his endeavours with them he was equally victorious, his services and skill, as a Military

Commander, attracted the notice of Government, and he was commissioned Major Gen of the U.S. Army in May 1812, and proceeded to the defence of New Orleans, and during the month of December 1814, he routed the British Troops in a number of skirmishes, in the vicinity of N Orleans. On the 8th Jan 1815, he totally defeated the British army of 9000 men in the memorable battle of N Orleans, leaving the British loss 2600 killed & wounded upon the field, the loss of the Americans being but 13 men, and their loss but 13 men being routed, he retired to his farm near Nashville Tenn in 1817 he was again called into the field, to suppress the seminoles of Florida, in 1821 was appointed Governor of Florida, in 1823 elected to the national senate, but being nominated for the presidency, resigned.

Elected President of the United States February 11th 1829, reelected in 1832

INAUGURAL ADDRESS.

Delivered on being sworn into office, March 4th 1829.

FELLOW CITIZENS,

About to undertake the arduous duties that I have been appointed to perform, by the choice of a free people, I avail myself of this customary and solemn occasion to express the gratitude which their confidence inspires and to acknowledge the accountability which my situation enjoined. While the magnitude of their interests convinces me, that no thanks can be adequate to the honor they have conferred, it admonishes me, that the best return that I can make is the zealous dedication of my humble abilities to their service and their good. As the instrument of the Federal constitution, it will devolve on me, for a stated period, to execute the laws of the United States, to superintend their foreign and their confederate relations, to manage their revenue, to command their forces, and by communications to the Legislature to watch over and to promote their interests generally. And the principles of action, by which I shall endeavour to accomplish this circle of duties, it is now proper for me to explain. In administering the laws of Congress, I shall keep steadily in view the limitations, as well as the extent, of the executive power, trusting thereby to discharge the functions of my office without transcending its authority. With foreign nations it will be my study to preserve peace, and to cultivate friendship on fair and honorable terms, and in the adjustment of any difference that may exist or arise, to exhibit the forbearance becoming a powerful nation, rather than the sensibility belonging to a gallant people. In such measures as I may be called upon to pursue, in regard to the rights of the separate states, I hope to be animated by a proper respect for those sovereign members of our Union, taking care not to confound the powers they have reserved to themselves, with those, they have granted to the confederacy. The management of the public revenue, that searching operation in all governments, is among the most delicate and important trusts in ours, and it will of course demand no inconsiderable share of my official solicitude. Under every aspect in which it can be considered, it would appear that advantage must result from the observance of a strict and faithful economy. This I shall aim at the more anxiously, both because it will facilitate the extinguishment of the national debt, the unnecessary duration of which is incompatible with real independence, and because it will counteract that tendency to public and private profligacy, which a profuse expenditure of money by the government is but too apt to engender. Powerful auxiliaries to the attainment of this desirable end, are to be found in the regulations, provided by the wisdom of Congress for the specific appropriations of the public money, and the prompt accountability of public officers. With regard to a proper selection of the subjects of impost, with a view to revenue, it would seem to me that the spirit of equity, caution & compromise, in which the constitution was framed, requires that the great interests of agriculture, commerce, and manufactures, should be equally favored, and that perhaps the only exceptions to this rule, should consist in the peculiar encouragement of any products of either of them, that may be found essential to our national independence. Internal improvement and the diffusion of knowledge, so far as they can be promoted by the constitutional acts of the Federal government, are of high importance. Considering standing armies as dangerous to free governments, in time of peace, I shall not seek to enlarge our present establishment, nor disregard that salutary lesson of political experience, which teaches that the military should be held subordinate to the civil power. The gradual increase of our Navy, whose flag has displayed in distant climes, our skill in navigation, and our fame in arms, the preservation of our forts, arsenals and dock yards, and the introduction of progressive improvements in the discipline and science of both branches of our military service, are so plainly prescribed by prudence that I should be excused for omitting their mention, sooner than for enlarging upon their importance. But the bulwark of our defence, is the national militia, which in the present state of our intelligence and population, must render us invincible. As long as our government is administered for the good of the people, and is regulated by their will, as long as it secures to us the rights of person, and of property, liberty of conscience, and freedom of the press, it will be worth defending, and so long as it is worth defending, a patriotic militia will cover it with an impenetrable ægis. Partial injuries and occasional mortifications, we may be subjected to, but a million of armed freemen, possessed of the means of war, can never be conquered by a foreign foe. To any just system, therefore, calculated to strengthen this natural safeguard of our country, I shall cheerfully lend all the aid in my power. It will be my sincere and constant desire, to observe toward the Indian tribes within our limits, a just and liberal policy, and to give that humane and considerate attention to their rights and their wants, which is consistent with the habits of our government, and the feelings of our people. The recent demonstration of public sentiment, inscribes on the list of executive duties, in characters too legible to be over looked, the task of reform, which will require particularly the correction of those abuses, that have brought the patronage of the Federal government into conflict with the freedom of elections, and the counteraction of those causes, which have disturbed the rightful course of appointment, and have placed, or continued power, in unfaithful or incompetent hands. In the performance of a task thus generally delineated, I shall endeavour to select men, whose diligence and talents will ensure in their respective stations, able and faithful cooperation, depending for the advancement of the public service, more on the integrity and zeal of the public officers, than on their numbers. A diffidence, perhaps too just, in my own qualifications, will teach me to look with reverence to the examples of public virtue, left by my illustrious predecessors, and with veneration, to the lights that flow from the mind that founded, and the mind that reformed our system. The same diffidence, induces me to hope for instruction, and aid from the coordinate branches of the government, and for the indulgence and support of my fellow citizens generally. And a firm reliance on the goodness of that power, whose providence mercifully protected our national infancy, and has since upheld our liberties in various vicissitudes, encourages me to offer up my ardent supplications, that he will continue to make our beloved country the object of his divine care, and gracious benediction.

Andrew Jackson

Above: Crowds pouring into the White House for Jackson's inaugural reception
Opposite page: Andrew Jackson's inaugural address

As thunderous cannon boomed and guns saluted him,
Jackson calmly got into a waiting carriage and rode down
Pennsylvania Avenue toward the White House. Veterans
of several wars lined both sides of the street, serving as
honor guards as the president passed. Then, forming a
long chain behind the carriage, the veterans followed him
to the White House as they had followed him to war.

At the White House, Jackson waited to meet people at an
informal reception. Refreshments were prepared for the
guests and everybody seemed ready for a well-organized
visit with the president. But once the crowd reached the
White House, they lost control. According to one writer,
"All sorts of people from the highest and most polished,
down to the most vulgar and gross in the nation" swarmed
in. They knocked over furniture and glassware and spilled
food and drink on satin-covered chairs.

This 1832 cartoon of Andrew Jackson portrays him as a vicious tyrant crushing the rights of the people.

Fearing for the president's safety, bodyguards hurried him out a side entrance to a nearby hotel. In the morning Jackson returned to the disrupted White House to begin an administration some called "The Reign of King Mob."

The United States was still a young country when Andrew Jackson was elected. With only twenty-four states in the Union, the country's official population was 12,866,020. Only white males could vote. Women, blacks, and other minorities had few rights. Though over 300,000 blacks had attained freedom by this time, over two million remained in slavery.

Cities were growing rapidly. With the arrival of millions of immigrants from Europe, problems of health and safety threatened the cities. Out in the country and along the coast, canals and steamboat lines were expanding trade

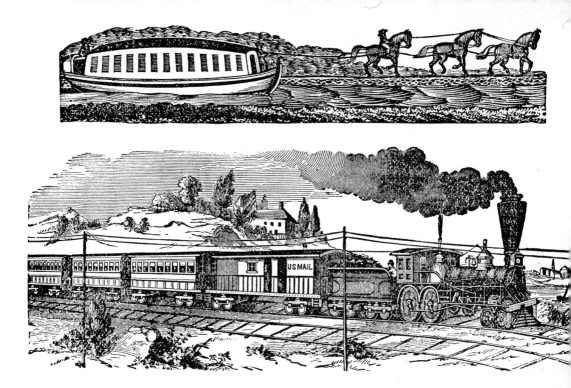

Above: A keelboat being towed upstream by a team of horses
Below: The railroad made it easy for people and goods to travel west.

and shortening the travel time between states. Experimentation with a steam engine set on rails was under way, and people were moving west to settle territories formerly claimed by Indians.

By 1833, citizens could buy a penny newspaper to learn the latest news. Through newspapers or public gatherings, most Americans kept informed of their frontier president. After all, he represented the American success story.

Born to poor, Scotch-Irish immigrants and raised in the Carolina backcountry, Jackson had become wealthy and attained the highest office in the land. He was the only president since George Washington without a college education. Andrew Jackson was proud of his humble beginnings. And he never strayed far from the common people who made it all possible for him.

Andrew Jackson (in doorway) was always ready to solve problems with his gun.

Chapter 2

Bully, Brawler, Soldier Boy

Attracted by the promise of a new life, Andrew Jackson's parents left northern Ireland for America in 1765. His father, also named Andrew, his mother Elizabeth Hutchinson, and his two infant brothers Hugh and Robert settled in a small farming community called the Waxhaw Region. It was 160 miles northwest of Charlestown, South Carolina, near the homes of Elizabeth's sisters and their husbands, the Crawfords.

After two years of exhausting labor, Mr. Jackson managed to build a small log cabin and bring in just enough crops to feed his family. The backbreaking work, however, took its toll on the tired man. In March 1767, he suddenly died, leaving behind his wife, pregnant with their third child, and his two sons—Hugh, age four, and Robert, age two. On March 15, 1767—only a few days after Elizabeth had buried her husband—she gave birth to Andrew, Junior.

Without her husband, Elizabeth was not able to support herself and her three children on their small farm. Before long, she moved in with the Crawfords and cared for the eight Crawford children as well as her own three.

Andrew Jackson's birthplace

Young Andrew grew up with more advantages than did his two older brothers. Hoping to see him become a Presbyterian minister, Elizabeth struggled to send him to better than common backcountry schools. But the ministry was the farthest thing from Andrew's mind. Mischievous and hot-tempered, he delighted in frightening and bullying other children.

Despite having had a better education than many boys his age, Andrew remained uninformed for most of his life. Though he was bright and could read at an early age, he refused to take his studies seriously. He preferred the wild and reckless freedom of fighting and playing. This early inattention to studies later gained him a reputation as one of the most poorly educated of American presidents.

Unlike earlier, well-educated presidents such as Jefferson, Madison, and the Adamses, Jackson relied more on his instincts and intuition. He knew little of history, geography, science, or literature. He could neither spell correctly

The signing of the Declaration of Independence

nor compose a proper sentence. Yet Jackson had a powerful writing style, and he could speak eloquently on subjects in which he truly believed.

Athletics rather than academics interested Andrew most during his early years. He had a deep love for horses — riding them and racing them. He was fond of foot races, jumping matches, and wrestling. Andrew thrived on competition. Those who competed against him quickly learned how important winning was to him. Easily offended, Andrew would never give up. And certainly, when he lost, he would never forget.

Much to his delight, Andrew's education was interrupted by the outbreak of war between the American colonists and Great Britain. He was nine years old in 1776 when delegates to the Second Continental Congress met in Philadelphia to sign the Declaration of Independence. Later, when the British attacked South Carolina, Andrew and his brothers joined the patriots to defend the colonies.

The first shot of the Revolution was fired at the Battle of Concord, Massachusetts

Taking up arms to defend their rights wasn't new to the Jackson boys. It was a long-standing family tradition. Often on cold winter evenings, Andrew and his brothers sat spellbound as their mother told chilling stories of the sufferings their grandfather had endured in Ireland under British rule. All the hatred their mother felt for those who oppressed others was quickly transferred to her sons. Throughout Andrew's life, he challenged anyone he believed was destroying the rights of others.

Thus, encouraged by their mother, the Jackson children courageously accepted their responsibility of "defending and supporting the rights of man." Andrew's oldest brother, Hugh, was the first to go to war. In 1779, at age sixteen, he joined a regiment and fought at the Battle of Stone Ferry. Duty called him only once, however. Immediately after the battle, Hugh died from excessive heat and fatigue.

In July of 1780 Andrew and Robert joined the mounted militia. Andrew, now only thirteen, may have done little

A British officer about to strike Andrew Jackson with his sword

more than tend to the troops and carry messages. Nevertheless, what he experienced in one year left a lasting impression. He carried the scars and the memories of the war all his life. They influenced both his military career and his career as president of the United States.

The war brought one tragedy after another to the Jackson family. On April 10, 1781, Andrew and his brother Robert took part in an exhausting skirmish with the Tories (pro-British colonists). Then, hungry and anxious, the two carelessly hid their horses and muskets in a thicket and ran to the home of their cousin Thomas Crawford. Before long, the Tories discovered the horses, surrounded the house, and barged in. It is said that Andrew angrily refused to obey an order to clean a British officer's boots. The officer struck Andrew with his sword, cutting his left hand to the bone and badly injuring his face and head. These scars remained for the rest of Jackson's life.

Andrew, Robert, their cousin Tom, and twenty other patriots were then taken to a prison in Camden, forty miles away. The boys were separated. Without proper food, water, and medicine, their wounds became infected and they soon burned with the fever of smallpox. Another week in prison and they might have died. Fortunately, an exchange of prisoners was taking place at this time. Mrs. Jackson, hearing that her sons were in Camden, had come from Waxhaw to plead with the British to include her sons in the prisoner exchange. She succeeded. On April 25 her sons and five Waxhaw neighbors were exchanged for thirteen British soldiers.

The forty-mile journey home was devastating. Mrs. Jackson placed Robert on one horse and she rode the other. Andrew walked, barefoot, bareheaded, and without a jacket. Somehow, they got home. Overcome with pain, the boys collapsed. Two days later Robert was dead and Andrew was delirious. Under a doctor's supervision and his mother's loving care, Andrew slowly recovered. When he had regained his strength, Mrs. Jackson left Andrew and joined other women who were going to Charlestown to care for prisoners of war. A few months after she began caring for her dying countrymen, Elizabeth Jackson became ill with cholera and died.

In November Andrew received a small package of his mother's belongings and was formally notified of her death. Although proud of his mother's extraordinary courage and devotion to duty, Andrew felt abandoned and alone. "I felt utterly alone," he said, "and tried to recall her last words to me."

Rachel Jackson's niece, Emily Donelson,
who took over duties as First Lady at
the White House when Rachel Jackson died

Andrew Jackson, Jr.,
Andrew and Rachel's adopted son

Sarah York Jackson,
wife of Andrew Jackson, Jr.

A portrait of Andrew Jackson by Thomas Sully

Jackson as a young soldier

Jackson as an old man

A frontier schoolhouse

Chapter 3

Frontier Fame and Fortune

After his mother died, Andrew wandered from relative to relative. For a short time he lived with his uncle, Thomas Crawford. But because he could not get along with others in the household, he left after only a month. His move into the home of Joseph White, another relative, was a bit more successful. Although Andrew suffered recurrent bouts of fever due to smallpox, he was able to overcome his illness and depression by working in White's saddle shop. Yet this, too, lasted only a short time. He became restless after six months and ran off with a group of boys from Waxhaw who liked to drink and gamble.

During this venture into horse-racing and cockfighting Andrew realized that he wanted to do more with his life. The serious side of Andrew led him back to school. For one year, possibly two, he even taught school. But at seventeen, teaching simply did not satisfy him. In December of 1784, he gathered his few belongings and rode seventy-five miles north to Salisbury, North Carolina, to become a lawyer.

Andrew found quarters in a small tavern called the Rowan House, where he met another law student named John McNairy. Spruce Macay, a distinguished lawyer, accepted Andrew as a student. For two years Andrew diligently read law books, copied papers, and ran errands. And each night after Macay's office closed, Andrew, John McNairy, and other law students "burned up" the town. Residents of Salisbury remarked that "Andrew Jackson was the most roaring, rollicking, game-cocking, horse-racing, card-playing, mischievous fellow that ever lived in Salisbury."

Late in 1786, for whatever reasons, Andrew thanked Macay for his training, packed his belongings once again, and went over to the office of Colonel John Stokes, one of the more brilliant lawyers of North Carolina. After six months under John Stokes's guidance, Andrew completed his legal training. On September 26, 1787, he appeared before two judges of the superior court for examination and was found to be "a man of unblemished moral character." The judges also authorized Andrew to practice law in the state of North Carolina.

Since there was little business for an inexperienced lawyer of twenty in Salisbury, Andrew drifted for a year from one county to the next, practicing law wherever he could. At the end of the year, Andrew's old friend John McNairy was elected superior court judge for the western district of North Carolina. This district stretched west to the Mississippi River and was dotted by little colonies of settlers. McNairy soon offered Andrew the post of public prosecutor for the district.

An eighteenth-century business office

Although the area was practically a wilderness, Andrew believed that many people heading west over the mountains would need help in their business affairs. Having a natural attraction to the West, and sensing that his opportunity had finally come, Andrew welcomed the adventure and accepted the post. Another friend, Thomas Searcy, accepted the office of clerk of court. Thus, McNairy, Jackson, Searcy, and other lawyer friends formed a law enforcement team and headed west together.

Early in 1788 the young men started out for Nashville, Tennessee, intending to bring law to the wilderness while making their own personal fortunes. They stopped first in Jonesborough, the largest town east of Nashville. The McNairy-Jackson team remained there for a few months, realizing that it would be foolish to make the two-hundred-mile journey to Nashville alone.

After organizing a larger party, the young lawyers arrived in the frontier town of Nashville on October 26, 1788. Then Andrew left his traveling companions and rode to the Donelson stockade to find lodging.

The Donelson family were some of the largest land-owners in the area. The head of the family was Rachel Stockley Donelson, widow of Colonel John Donelson, who had led an expedition of settlers across the Cumberland Gap in 1779. Rachel took in male boarders at the stockade for protection. These men slept in log cabin rooms near the blockhouse and ate their meals with the family. The Donelsons took a liking to Andrew and gave him a room to share with John Overton, a friend Andrew would admire all of his life. Immediately, the two young lawyers set up a private law office in their tiny room.

Before long, a firm bond of friendship developed between Andrew and the Donelson boys. During his visits Andrew became attracted to Mrs. Donelson's daughter, also named Rachel, who at twenty-one was an excellent horse rider, a gifted storyteller, and a singer. Rachel smoked a corncob pipe, not an uncommon habit for frontier women at this time, and delighted everyone with her fun-loving nature. Although Rachel was already married, she could not resist the attraction of the tall, red-haired Jackson gentleman.

As the days passed, Andrew learned of Rachel's unhappy marriage at age seventeen to Captain Lewis Robards, an intensely jealous man. After many violent quarrels, Rachel and her husband had separated for a while. At the time Andrew came to live with the Donelsons, Rachel and her

Rachel Jackson

husband had just decided to resume their marriage. They were living with her mother while waiting for their house to be built five miles away. The gallant Andrew, wishing to protect Rachel from her abusive husband, confronted Robards about his treatment of Rachel. After a particularly threatening incident with Robards, Andrew moved out of the Donelson home. Robards soon moved out also.

For the next two years Andrew saw Rachel regularly. In the spring of 1791, John Overton brought news that Lewis Robards had been granted a divorce from Rachel. Pleased by the news, Andrew announced that he would marry her in the fall. In all the excitement, however, he forgot to obtain legal proof of Rachel's divorce. This unfortunate mistake caused painful problems for them later when Andrew ran for political office.

A drawing of the Hermitage, the Jacksons' plantation near Nashville

Rachel and Andrew were both twenty-four years old when they married. That same year, the territorial governor of Tennessee appointed Andrew attorney general. Everything seemed to be going well for Jacksons until about two years later, when they learned that Rachel had not actually been divorced in 1791. Lewis Robards had brought suit against Rachel in 1791, but the divorce was not finalized until two years later. Andrew and Rachel were shocked at the thought that she had been married to two men at the same time. Hoping that such a scandal would be forgotten in time, they were quietly remarried on January 17, 1794.

Original cabins on the Hermitage grounds

Andrew Jackson's marriage to Rachel tied him to one of the largest and most influential families in Tennessee. But though the marriage brought him immediate social recognition, Jackson had already built a reputation as a successful frontier lawyer. A man of tireless energy, Jackson won most of his cases, which involved sales, land disputes, debts, and assault and battery.

Since there was little cash in circulation on the frontier at this time, Jackson's clients often paid him in whiskey, cotton, slaves, and land. Jackson gladly accepted land in payment for his services. In fact, by the time Tennessee became a state in 1796, Jackson had become quite an extensive landowner with all the slaves and slave-trade dealings that went with the position. He had built a 650-acre plantation twelve miles from Nashville, which he fondly called the Hermitage.

In the fall of 1796, Jackson was elected Tennessee's only representative to the United States Congress. He arrived in Philadelphia, then the nation's capital and a city of 65,000 people, just as George Washington was leaving office and John Adams was settling in.

Jackson's first official business as a congressman was to vote on a statement that praised the accomplishments of the retiring president. When the vote was called, Jackson voted "nay." He did not approve of the direction Washington had given the new nation. First of all, he did not agree with some of Washington's foreign policies toward Great Britain. Also, he believed that Washington's treaties with the Indians interfered with the claims of white settlers. Jackson's vote disturbed many in Congress. His bold rejection of the man revered as the "Father of the Country" was considered disrespectful.

As disturbing as Jackson was to some members in Congress, many more people back home in Tennessee approved of his frontier stand on their behalf. For instance, Jackson had introduced a bill in Congress to reimburse Tennessee for losses in its war against the Cherokee Indians. The ink was not quite dry on the bill when grateful Tennesseeans elected him senator.

But Jackson seemed unsuited for the Senate. He was young, inexperienced, and distracted by his own personal business affairs. Bored, unhappy, and very disappointed with John Adams's administration, Jackson obtained a leave of absence from the Senate in April 1798. Returning to Nashville, after serving only one session in Congress, Jackson resigned his Senate seat.

Judge Jackson arresting a desperado

That same year, at the age of thirty-one, Jackson was elected judge of the superior court of Tennessee—a post that carried a salary of $600 a year. He served on the bench for six years, holding court in Knoxville, Jonesborough, and Nashville. Jackson made an excellent backwoods judge. He spoke without fear or hesitation and delivered his decisions swiftly. Besides, wearing a black robe and keeping two loaded pistols on his desk, he conducted a very orderly court.

Jackson was known for his fierce sense of justice and fairness in the courtroom. He was a man of the highest integrity. An early biographer observed "that he maintained the dignity and authority of the bench; and that his decisions were short, untechnical, unlearned, sometimes ungrammatical, and generally right."

Jackson's courtroom behavior did not always carry over into his personal life. His rugged frontier experience taught him to settle most personal grievances with a gun. During his lifetime, Jackson came close to carrying out six duels to protect his honor and Rachel's good name. In 1797 he challenged Governor John Sevier and his old friend Judge John McNairy to duels, although neither duel was fought. A duel in 1806 with Charles Dickinson, known by many as the best shot in Tennessee, left Jackson severely wounded and Dickinson dead.

Upon the advice of John Overton, Jackson was to let Dickinson fire first. That's what Jackson did. Dickinson aimed directly for Jackson's heart but misjudged because of the loose-fitting coat Jackson wore. (Many believe that Jackson wore this oversized coat purposely to mislead Dickinson.)

The bullet struck Jackson in the chest, shattering two ribs slightly below the heart. Clenching his teeth in pain, Jackson grabbed his throbbing chest and steadied himself. Now it was his turn. Aiming slowly and deliberately, Jackson fired. His first shot misfired. The second one went right through Dickinson's body, just below the ribs. Dickinson fell. As Jackson walked away, in a shoe filled with blood, Charles Dickinson bled to death at the feet of his surprised friends. For more than a month Jackson suffered from the wound. The bullet, lodged dangerously close to his heart, was never removed. He carried the bullet and the memory of the duel all his life.

Opposite page: Jackson in a loose-fitting coat

The cotton gin, invented by Eli Whitney

Jackson had time to recuperate from his injury, since he no longer held public office. He had returned to private life in 1804 after resigning as judge and failing to win an appointment as governor of Tennessee.

Free from the burdens of political life, Andrew and Rachel began putting their energies into improving their land. With one of only twenty-four plantations in the country that owned a cotton gin, the Jacksons increased their own cotton yields and serviced their neighbors' plantations as well. During their more prosperous years, they had 150 slaves working their fields. They grew cotton, corn, and wheat and raised cows, mules, pigs, and horses.

For a time Jackson and two partners operated a general store, tavern, and stables. They traded with a New Orleans

Slaves picking cotton on a Southern plantation

market and, as a sideline, also built riverboats for other traders. But due to bad debts and Jackson's poor business skills, the business failed. Fortunately, Jackson had other sources of income, and he could always rely on Rachel's excellent management of the Hermitage to bring them through the discouraging times of bankruptcy.

Rachel and Andrew never had any children of their own. However, Rachel's brother Severn Donelson allowed them to adopt one of his twin boys in 1810 and raise him as their own. The Jacksons christened the baby Andrew, Junior. Young Andrew brought much joy to Rachel, especially during the long, lonely days when Jackson was away. Several years later another nephew, Andrew Jackson Donelson, also came to live with them.

Left: This is the picture of Rachel Jackson that Andrew wore around his neck on a beaded chain after she died.
Before his own death, he gave it to his granddaughter, also named Rachel Jackson.

Below: A bedroom in the Hermitage, called the Lafayette Room

Right: Rachel Jackson, who died during Jackson's 1828 presidential campaign

Mᴿˢ RACHEL JACKSON
late Consort to
ANDREW JACKSON,
President of the U. States

Below: The Jackson family graveyard at the Hermitage

Chapter 4

Tough As Old Hickory

In 1812 a new challenge confronted the Jacksons. Andrew became involved in a war that would completely change the direction of their lives. Since 1804 Great Britain had been seizing American ships on the open seas, confiscating their cargoes, and kidnapping the sailors to serve on British ships in their war against France. In addition, westerners were angered because the British had been siding with the Indians in battles with Americans in the Northwest Territories. Finally, the United States declared war. This came to be known as the War of 1812.

Eagerly accepting his country's call to arms, Andrew left behind his life-style as country gentleman. Now at age forty-five, he assumed command of two thousand Tennessee volunteers. Although the American plan of attack called for the invasion of Canada, which was British territory at the time, Jackson was ordered south to Pensacola, Florida. Florida belonged to Spain in 1812, and the Spanish government was allowing the British navy free access to its ports.

Jackson and his men in Pensacola, Florida

It was winter when Jackson marched his troops more than five hundred miles to Natchez, in Mississippi Territory, where he awaited further orders. Weeks later, when he finally received word that the invasion had been canceled and he was to dismiss his troops, Jackson became furious. How could the government expect his men to make their way home without pay, food, or medicine?

Concerned for his soldiers' comfort and safety, Jackson borrowed money to buy wagons and supplies for their return home. It was then that Jackson's men began calling him "Old Hickory." Since hickory wood was the toughest living thing these frontiersmen knew, they called their leader "Old Hickory" as a tribute to his courage.

General Jackson arrived home with his worn troops in May of 1813. A few months later he had a new government commission—to defeat the Creek Indians living in

Jackson with Chief Red Eagle (William Weatherford) after the Creek War

Mississippi Territory. The Creeks had allied themselves with the remarkable Shawnee chief Tecumseh and his brother Tenskwatawa. Together they plotted to push Americans back to the coast. Tecumseh believed that if he organized the various tribes into a powerful confederation and joined forces with the British, the Indians could drive Americans from the region and reclaim their native lands.

Many Indians supported Tecumseh's plan. Black Hawk of the Sauks came east from Rock Island to join the struggle. Chief Red Eagle, also known as William Weatherford, led the Creeks. Unfortunately, Tecumseh underestimated the Americans and misjudged General Andrew Jackson. Jackson's counterattack was so overwhelming that all tribes east of the Mississippi River eventually would be driven out.

Shawnee Chief Tecumseh

Although Tecumseh played a leading role in the war, his efforts were short lived. He died in the Battle of the Thames in 1813, before the Indians could put up any significant resistance.

By October 1813, Jackson had gathered several thousand volunteers to pursue the Creeks. A few months earlier these Indians had killed four hundred settlers at Fort Mims, a stronghold near the Florida border. It was common knowledge that the British were sending guns upcountry from Pensacola to aid the Creeks. Although weak and pale from a bullet wound he had suffered during a tavern brawl, Jackson mustered his strength and marched his volunteers toward Alabama. He planned to teach the Creeks a lesson they would never forget.

Left: Davy Crockett   **Right: Sam Houston**

Among Jackson's dedicated volunteers were such famous fighters as Davy Crockett and Sam Houston. Yet his Indian campaign was not without its problems. Jackson still suffered from his recent bullet wound, which had never fully healed. Then he contracted dysentery. His troops came close to starvation and mutiny several times. With each new setback, however, Jackson became more firmly resolved to meet problems head-on.

Newspapers often attacked Jackson's conduct during the war. They criticized his orders to shoot an eighteen-year-old soldier who had disobeyed an officer. They were outraged further by his orders to have several soldiers shot to death. After a brief trial, these men had been convicted of stealing supplies from a storehouse and trying to enlist hundreds of soldiers to mutiny.

A TRIBUTE TO MERIT.

Briga Gen A Coffee is invited to partake
of a PUBLIC DINNER, to be given by the citizens of Nashville and its vicinity, to MAJ.
GEN. ANDREW JACKSON, at the Nashville Inn, on Thursday, the 19th inst. as a proof
of their decided approbation of the gallant and meritorious manner, in which he has conducted
and terminated the Creek War.

DINNER on the Table at 3 o'clock.

John Childress,
Geo. M Deaderick,
Jno. Sommerville,
John Bod,
Alexander Richardson,   } Committee.
Roger B. Sappington,
Ephraim Pritchett,
Andrew Hynes,
James Jackson.

May 12, 1814.

An invitation to a dinner honoring Jackson after the Creek War

With his commanding presence and his iron will,
Jackson demanded obedience from his men, even under
terrible adversity. During heated battles against the
Creeks, said a biographer, "he was seen . . . rallying the
alarmed, halting them in their flight, forming his col-
umns, and inspiriting them by his example."

The Battle of Horseshoe Bend was the turning point in
the Creek uprising. Jackson's victory over the Creeks
broke their spirit. On the morning of March 27, 1814,
Jackson and several thousand fresh troops surprised the
Creeks encamped near the Tallapoosa River. Though
severely outnumbered, the Creeks refused to surrender.
The brutal slaughter continued until nightfall. On the
following morning over 600 Creeks lay dead. Jackson's
losses numbered only 55 killed and 146 wounded.

Red Eagle, leader of the Creeks, was absent from the
village when Jackson attacked. A few days later he boldly
rode into Jackson's camp and demanded to see him. During their meeting, Red Eagle persuaded Jackson to feed the

44

The Creek Chief Shelocta appealed to Jackson to spare Creek lands.

surviving Creek women and children. He in turn promised to convince other Creeks to give up war. Red Eagle later settled on a small plantation in Alabama, though he was never completely safe from enemies.

For his successful campaign against the Creeks, Jackson was awarded the rank of major general. The position carried with it a yearly salary of $6,500 and command of the Seventh Military District. A vast area, this included the territories of Tennessee, Louisiana, and Mississippi.

Exercising the authority of his newly acquired rank, Jackson called together the Creek chiefs at Fort Jackson on August 10, 1814, to discuss treaty terms. Not much discussion was allowed, however. Jackson demanded that the Creeks turn over twenty-three million acres of land to the United States government. (This included three-fifths of what is now the state of Alabama and one-fifth of Georgia.) With no alternative, the Creeks signed the cruel treaty and began moving their camps.

The British burn Washington, D.C.

Because of Jackson's demands in the Treaty of Fort Jackson, vast Indian lands opened to settlers. This made Jackson a hero throughout the South and West. As for the Creeks, their nation was completely destroyed.

In other areas of the war, things were not going as well for the Americans. On August 24, 1814, the British marched into Washington, D.C., and burned the president's mansion. President James Madison and his wife, Dolley, escaped with a few cherished paintings from the Capitol building before it, too, was burned. Then rumors began of a second British invasion, through Florida.

Jackson's headquarters in New Orleans

When news of the impending invasion reached Jackson, he hurried his army south. After strengthening Fort Boyer in Mobile, he stormed into Pensacola on the heels of the fleeing British. Then he raced his army back to Mobile, expecting the British to invade there. When the British failed to show up after ten days, Jackson promptly turned west. His intuition told him that the British would invade through New Orleans.

Arriving there on December 2, 1814, General Jackson immediately began closing off the city. His troops felled trees to clog the bayous (water routes through the swamps) and erected cannon at Fort Saint Phillip on the Mississippi River. A squadron of five small gunboats also began patrolling Lake Borgne.

47

The pirate
Jean Laffite

In the meantime Jackson began enlisting more troops, collecting a strange assortment of men to join his Tennesseans. Genteel New Orleans militiamen joined his ranks, alongside Choctaw Indians, several hundred free blacks, and a band of notorious pirates led by the Laffite brothers. The backbone of the army, however, consisted of the fearsome "Kaintucks"—frontiersmen from Kentucky and other wild territory up the Mississippi River.

Each Kaintuck looked like a walking arsenal, complete with scalping knife, tomahawk, hunting knife, whiskey bottle, and long rifle. While the regular army soldier used a short-range musket, the Kaintuck's long rifle could outshoot any musket by a hundred yards. He made his rifle even deadlier by using "buck and ball"—two small buckshot pellets in addition to the normal bullet.

A frontier soldier

Although the Kaintucks were greatly respected for their marksmanship, the "townbred" soldiers did not like associating with them. Some said that Kaintucks stank so badly you couldn't stand downwind of them. It was also said that "a Kaintuck would sooner go hungry than do without his whiskey bottle." Actually, for the rugged frontiersman, whiskey was the closet thing to medicine he could get. According to one writer, "whiskey warmed their insides during the dank, cold winters, and there was nothing like it for aching bones and rotting teeth."

Jackson's men battle the British at New Orleans

When 6,000 British troops invaded New Orleans on December 23, Jackson's 2,200 soldiers were ready for them. For over two weeks they engaged in sporadic battle. Then on the morning of January 8, 1815, the British attacked the Americans in the final battle of New Orleans—a battle that should never have taken place.

When British soldiers marched forward into four lines of American sharpshooters, bodies fell like rain. At noon, after the smoke of the battle had cleared, there were over two thousand British casualties. Only fourteen Americans had been killed. What neither side knew was that, fifteen days earlier, a peace treaty between the United States and Great Britain had been signed, ending the War of 1812. The news did not reach America until February.

Meanwhile, Jackson's astonishing victory at New Orleans shocked both sides. For ten days after the battle, both armies buried their dead and kept an uneasy watch on each other. On January 19, the remaining British troops retreated to their ships and shamefully sailed away. A few days later, the American army marched into New Orleans in triumph, amid the peal of church bells and the unrestrained cheers of a jubilant crowd.

In Washington, it was said, people went "wild with delight." The stunning victory restored pride and confidence among Americans. Patriotic refrains could be heard throughout the states. People defiantly asked, "Who would not be an American?" and then boldly replied, "Long live the Republic!"

For Andrew Jackson this was a glorious time. The nation needed a hero just when he had the ability and the desire to become one. Congress honored Jackson with a gold medal, and President James Madison voiced the gratitude of the country: "History records no example of such a glorious victory, obtained with so little bloodshed on the part of the victorious."

Jackson is hailed as the Hero of New Orleans

A Seminole Indian family in Florida

The war at an end, Jackson—lonely for Rachel and his son—returned to the Hermitage. A magnificent public reception awaited him. Among the guests was Thomas Jefferson, then seventy-two years of age. Jefferson toasted Jackson with the words "Honor and gratitude to those who have filled the measure of their country's honor."

Overwhelmed by the spirit and response of the American people, Jackson began touring the country to give them a glimpse of their brave hero. But no sooner had Jackson tasted the glory of a traveling hero than the call to duty sounded again. This time it involved the Seminole Indians in Spanish-owned Florida.

Driven south into Florida, the Seminoles had begun hunting in Georgia in deliberate violation of the Treaty of Fort Jackson. This concerned Andrew Jackson; he feared that Florida was becoming a training ground for Indian raids as well as a home for runaway black slaves. The alliance of two such dissatisfied groups could develop into

Billy Bowlegs, chief of the Seminoles

a force that would be difficult to control. Also, settlers had begun moving into Florida, and violence began to break out between them and the Seminoles.

President Monroe sent Jackson a letter with vague instructions to "repair to the command of the troops now acting against the Seminoles, a tribe which has long violated our rights and insulted our national character." Assuming that this gave him full authority for an invasion, Jackson pursued the Seminoles into Florida.

On route to the camp of Chief Bowlegs, leader of the Seminoles, Jackson burned several Seminole villages and killed the people there. But he never succeeded in apprehending Chief Bowlegs. Forewarned by British friends, Bowlegs and his people had disappeared into the swamps before Jackson arrived. Once in the abandoned camp, however, Jackson found two British citizens who had been encouraging Seminoles to fight the Americans.

Jackson quells a mutiny during his Florida campaign

He had them killed. Then, disregarding further international concerns, Jackson turned his attention to the Spanish. First he captured the fort of Saint Mark's. Then, arriving in Pensacola on May 24, Jackson threw out the Spanish governor and boldly claimed the territory for the United States.

Jackson's actions in Florida had serious repercussions in Washington. United States diplomats found themselves in the embarrassing position of repairing relations with England and Spain. Fortunately for America, the British did not regard Jackson's killing of two of its citizens as a major incident. Still smarting from its defeat at New Orleans, England avoided any new cause for war. And the Spanish, after extensive negotiations with Secretary of State John Quincy Adams, decided to rid themselves of the

The capture of Osceola, leader of the Seminole warriors

troublesome territory of Florida. They ceded it to the United States in exchange for the five million dollars' worth of claims that American citizens held against Spain for damages during the Indian raids.

Thus, what could have been an international problem became instead an opportunity for national prominence and expansion. With the Indians' power broken in the Northwest Territory and General Andrew Jackson's commanding leadership in the South, the United States proclaimed to the world a kind of second Declaration of Independence. No longer would rumors be heard that America would eventually return to British rule. But, more importantly, America proudly extended its empire and established itself as a power other nations would soon learn to respect.

Newly-elected President Jackson, on his way to Washington

Chapter 5

Birth of the Democratic Party

After his victory at New Orleans, Andrew Jackson seemed to gain national prominence overnight. For a while he made the most of his popularity by touring the major cities of Baltimore, Philadelphia, and New York—no doubt seeking the approval of eastern Americans just as he had done in the West. But Jackson found no political opportunity in the East just yet. Instead he was appointed military governor of Florida.

Jackson moved his family to Florida but resigned the governorship after serving only one year. Unhappy and sickly, Jackson brought his family back home to Tennessee. There John Overton and other congressional friends began grooming Jackson for the presidency. Through their efforts he was elected senator from Tennessee, a position he had held twenty-six years earlier. Then, thanks to the political maneuvers of Martin Van Buren, the junior senator from New York, Jackson was formally nominated for the presidency. Although John Quincy Adams, William H. Crawford, and Henry Clay were also running for the office, Americans voiced their choice of Jackson.

Top left: Martin Van Buren,
Jackson's campaign manager

Above: South Carolina
Senator John C. Calhoun

Left: Missouri Senator
Thomas Hart Benton

However, presidential elections are determined by the electoral vote, not the popular vote. Although Jackson was the obvious choice of the people, he did not receive the electoral votes necessary to become president. It was John Quincy Adams who won the office and became sixth president of the United States.

Shortly after the votes were tabulated and Jackson's loss became official, he and his supporters began preparing for the 1828 election. This time they would win. Martin Van Buren became Jackson's campaign manager. His first priority was to gain the support of Senator John C. Calhoun of South Carolina and Senator Thomas Hart Benton of Missouri. Together they began organizing a new political party from the ground up. Realizing that they needed a different approach to the election, they created a new campaign style for Jackson.

They introduced catchy songs and slogans into the campaign to bring attention to Jackson. Bands, dinners, and rallies were held to gain support. Gimmicks such as buttons and clothes were distributed to show voting preference. Newspapers brought the widest publicity. Through cartoons and written reports, Jacksonians began publishing Jackson's accomplishments and downgrading John Quincy Adams.

As the campaign picked up momentum, Jackson supporters called themselves Democratic-Republicans. They chose hickory as a symbol of their candidate and their party. Before long, hickory sticks, hickory canes, and hickory brooms became popular items across the country. New public interest was aroused.

Jackson supporters rallying around a hickory pole

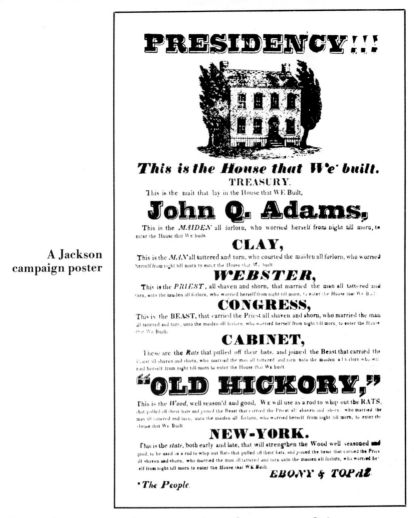

Soon, however, the campaign degenerated into name-calling on both sides. The candidates as well as their wives were accused of adultery, theft, even murder. Newspapers reported every accusation in detail, and people crowded to the polls by the thousands.

Since the western states were allowing all white males to vote in 1828, regardless of property ownership, voter turnout was nearly three times what it had been in the election of 1824. When returns were counted, Jackson claimed victory with 647,286 of the popular vote to Adams's 508,064. Jackson clinched the election with 178 electoral votes to Adams's 83.

The White House during Jackson's time

But the bitterly waged campaign took its toll on the Jacksons. Rachel Jackson never quite recovered from the abuses aimed at her during the campaign. On December 17, 1828, just three months before Jackson was to take office, she suffered a heart attack and died. Jackson was heartbroken. He grieved for weeks. Finally, about mid-January, he regained his control and left for Washington. He was accompanied by his nephew Andrew Jackson Donelson, who would serve as his private secretary, and Donelson's wife, Emily, who would function as First Lady.

Being the first president to come from a poor family west of the Appalachian Mountains, Jackson received his greatest support from the common people. He tried throughout his administration to form government decisions and legislation with them in mind. As his first order

A political cartoon making fun of Jackson's policy of awarding public offices, or "spoils," to those who helped him win the 1828 campaign.

of business upon taking office, Jackson replaced Adams's government employees with common people who had supported him. He believed that common people should have the opportunity to hold office as well as to vote. This method of rotating office holders came to be known as the "spoils system."

Most of the people Jackson appointed to his cabinet—with the exception of his secretary of state, Martin Van Buren—were undistinguished men. Jackson preferred the advice of men who were in touch with the common people. Several western newspaper editors formed the core of Jackson's advisers. This group later became known as the "kitchen cabinet" because it was said that these advisers slipped into the White House through the back entrance to see the president.

A toll gate on the Maysville Turnpike

Jackson's belief that he was the voice of the people led him to veto more legislation than all previous presidents combined. The first of his vetoes was against federal construction of the Maysville Road in Kentucky. Jackson felt that it was the state of Kentucky's responsibility to finance this road. Although this decision did not favor Kentucky, Jackson usually sided with the states on land rights issues—particularly when Indians were involved.

Over the years, the steady push of Americans west and south had driven about 53,000 Cherokee, Creek, Choctaw, and Chickasaw Indians onto 33 million acres of prized territory. By the 1820s Americans were beginning to settle in this land. The problem of what to do with Indians who had the first rights to the land became an issue. Most Easterners believed that Indians should be assimilated, or taught to live as other Americans lived. But Andrew Jackson and the Westerners believed that Indians blocked American expansion and that it would be better to remove them.

John Ross, chief of the Cherokees

Jackson honestly believed that it would be best to move all the Indians west of the Mississippi River to an area that the government would provide for them. He wrote, "Where they now are they and my white children are too near to each other to live in harmony and peace."

President Jackson believed that the new Indian land would be better for farming and would provide more game for hunting. Indians there would be guaranteed protection forever against white settlement. Adequate supplies would be given them for the journey west, and provisions would be supplied for a year after their arrival in the new land. What Jackson completely overlooked, however, was the well-established way of life the Indians would have to abandon. He cared nothing for their need to remain where their ancestors were buried.

Sequoyah, inventor of the Cherokee alphabet

The Cherokee were the most advanced tribe of Indians east of the Mississippi. According to a census taken in 1825, the Cherokee owned 33 grist mills, 13 sawmills, 1 powder mill, 69 blacksmith shops, 2 tan yards, 762 looms, 2,486 spinning wheels, 172 wagons, 2,923 plows, 7,683 horses, 22,531 black cattle, 46,732 pigs, and 2,566 sheep. They had been using a system of writing developed by a Cherokee named Sequoyah and had been publishing a newspaper in their own language since 1821. They operated schools, a mounted police force, and a government modeled after that of the United States.

Because the Cherokee had made treaties with the U.S. government, they thought they would be protected from removal. After all, the U.S. government had always considered them a separate nation. The Hopewell Treaty of 1785, the Treaty and Intercourse Act of 1802, and eleven other treaties up to 1819 had placed them outside the jurisdiction of state laws. But in 1828 Georgia passed a bill

A copy of the court proceedings in the case of the Cherokee Nation against the state of Georgia after Cherokee lands in Georgia were taken

that allowed the Georgia government to divide all Cherokee territory in the state into parcels and place it under Georgia counties. The counties in turn could open it to white settlement. In 1829 another act abolished all Cherokee laws and declared that no Cherokee could testify in court against a white man.

The Cherokee Nation responded by filing two lawsuits against the state of Georgia—one in 1831 and one in 1832. The ruling of Supreme Court Justice John Marshall favored Cherokee rights to disregard Georgia state laws. Unfortunately, Georgia disregarded Marshall's ruling and President Jackson did nothing to enforce it. He told the Cherokees: "States have been created within your ancient limits, which claim a right to govern and control your people as they do their own citizens, and to make them answerable to their civil and criminal codes. Your great father [Jackson] has not the authority to prevent this state of things."

The Sauk Chief Black Hawk

Jackson's decision to support Georgia's state rights over the Indians' rights left the Cherokee no alternative but to fight or submit. The Indian Removal Act of 1830, followed by the Indian Intercourse Act of 1834, put the final cap on Indian occupied land. Through these acts, lands held by Indians in all twenty-four states were to be exchanged for new lands west of the Mississippi River. This new land, called Indian Territory, later became the state of Oklahoma.

The Indian Removal Act had its opponents in Congress. For nearly two months prior to its passage, a debate over the bill raged. Congressman David Crockett of Tennessee opposed the bill, and senators from New Jersey and Massachusetts argued six hours against its passage. Eventually all efforts to stall Indian removal were blocked. The bill passed the Senate 28 to 19 and the House of Representatives 102 to 97. In 1831 removal began.

The Battle of Bad Axe

Although the president wished removal to be voluntary, "for it would be as cruel as unjust to compel them to abandon the graves of their fathers and seek a home in a distant land," most tribes were unwilling to leave. Removal became harsh and often brutal. Creeks in Alabama were removed in chains. Choctaws were forced from Mississippi in winter without proper clothing or provisions.

In the winter of 1831, Black Hawk, a Sauk chief, and his people were forced from their village in Illinois and marched west into Iowa. When spring came, about a thousand hungry Indians recrossed the Mississippi to plant grain on their former farms. White settlers, suspecting an attack (or perhaps just looking for an excuse), slaughtered the Indians. Black Hawk and many of his followers fled. Followed for hundreds of miles, they were finally cornered near the Bad Axe River in Wisconsin. Despite a flag of truce, most of the Indians were killed. Black Hawk escaped but later surrendered. He was imprisoned at a fort in Missouri, where he later died. History records this incident as the Black Hawk War of 1832.

Thousands of Indians lost their lives along the "Trail of Tears."

In 1835 the Seminole in Florida faced a similar fate. Led by Osceola, and aided by escaped black slaves, the Seminole fought guerrilla-style warfare in the swampy grasslands known as the everglades. But seven years and fifteen million dollars later, the U.S. government defeated them and most were driven west. Osceola died in prison.

Eventually even the Cherokee Nation yielded to the president. Although most Cherokee, under Chief John Ross, opposed relocation, the Cherokee Removal—often called "The Trail of Tears"—began in 1838. By the winter of 1839, between thirteen thousand and seventeen thousand Cherokee were forced west under armed guard. They traveled eight hundred miles in steamboats, in railroad cars, and on foot. Along the way, outlaws made off with their livestock and stole much of their money. Disease and starvation reduced their numbers. Many suffocated in railroad cars. In all, the Cherokee buried onefourth of their nation along the way to a promised land that was far inferior to the land they left.

During his administration Jackson signed more than ninety removal treaties, promising lands in the west that they could keep forever. "There," he said, "their white brethren will not trouble them . . . and they can live upon it, they and all their children as long as grass grows or water runs in peace and plenty."

But the president told a slightly different story to Congress. He told them that "whenever the safety, interest or defense of the country" is at stake, Congress can "occupy and possess any part of Indian territory." Occupy and possess they did. By the time Jackson left office, most Indian treaties had already been broken. During his eight years as president, an estimated 100 million acres of land had been taken from various tribes. Only 32 million acres had been set aside for the nearly 46,000 Indians who were removed west of the Mississippi River.

Eventually Jackson's policy of Indian removal won acceptance by most Americans. Although a few were outraged by it and some felt uncomfortable about how removal was handled, many Americans were not even concerned. Most admitted that it was probably the only possible solution to the "Indian problem."

Some Account of some of the Bloody Deeds
OF
GENERAL JACKSON.

Jacob Webb   David Morrow   John Harris   Henry Lewis   David Hunt   Edward Lindsey

A true Account of the Execution of the Six Militia Men.

As we may soon expect to have the official documents in relation to the Six Militia Men, arrested, tried, and put to death, under the orders of General Andrew Jackson, this may not be an improper time to give to the public some of the particulars of their execution, as we have them from "AN EYE WITNESS," who appeals to Col. Russell, for the truth of every word he relates.

Harris was a Baptist preacher, with a large family. He had hired as a substitute for three months. This was the case with most of them. They were ignorant men, but obstinate in what they believed right, and what they had been told by their officers was right.— They were all sure they could not be kept beyond three months, and they gave up their musquets, and had provisions dealt out to them, from the public stores, before they left the camp.— This confirmed their convictions that they were right and doing what was lawful.

Col. Russel commanded at the execution. The Militia men were brought to the place in a large wagon. The military dispositions being made, Col. Russell rode up to the wagon and ordered the men to descend. Harris was

the only one who betrayed feminine weakness. The awfulness of the occasion; his wife and nine children; the parting with his son; and the fear of a quickly approaching ignominious death' quite overcome him, and he sunk in unmanly grief. No feeling of military pride could brace him up.

Col. Russel, doubtless, felt as a man, but he felt also for the pride of the army, and desired to animate the men with fortitude. "You are about to die, said he, by the sentence of a Court Martial—die like men; like soldiers You have been brave in the field—'tis you have fought well—do no discredit it to your country, or dishonour to the army, or yourselves, by any unmanly fears. Meet your fate with courage."

Harris attempted to make some apology for his conduct, but while he spoke, he wept bitterly. The fear of death, the idea that he should never again behold his wife and little ones, and his son weeping near him, had taken such entire possession of his mind that it was impossible he should rally.

Lewis, the gallant Lewis, said in a clear and manly tone, "Colonel, I have served my country well. I love it dearly, and would, if I could, serve it longer and better. I have fought bravely—you know I have, and so am I have a right to say so myself.

"would not wish to die in this way"— here his voice faltered, and he passed the back of his right hand over his eyes —"I did not expect it. But, I am now "as firm as I have been in battle, and "you shall see that I will die as be- "comes a soldier, you know I am a "brave man." "Yes, Lewis, said the Colonel, you have always behaved like a brave man." Other sentences were uttered, other declarations were made, and words of comfort spoken, but they were lost on me: my attention, says an Eye Witness, being chiefly directed to Lewis.

Six coffins were ranged as directed, and on each of them knelt one of our condemned American Militia Men— Such a sight was never seen before! I trust to God it never will be seen again! Six soldiers were detailed and drawn up to fire at each man. What an awful duty! Their white caps were drawn over the faces of the unhappy men.— Harris evidently trembled, and I could almost persuade myself that the heart of Lewis was enlarged, and that his bosom rose with manly courage to meet death. The fatal word was given and they all fell.

As we approached the scene of blood and carnage, Lewis gave signs of life; the rest were all dead—he crawled up on his coffin. After the lapse of a few

minutes he said—I give his very words. "Colonel"—the Colonel was close to him—"Colonel, I am not killed, but I am sadly cut and mangled." His body was now examined and it was found that but four balls had wounded him. "Colonel," said I, "did I behave well." "Yes, Lewis," said the Colonel in the kindest tone of voice—"like a man." "Well sir," said he, "have I not atoned for this offence? Shall I not live?" The Colonel was much agitated, and gave orders that the Surgeon should if possible, preserve his life. They did all that skill and humanity could do— it was all of no avail. Poor Lewis ran present a great desire to live—"not," said he at one time, "that I fear death, "but I would repent me of some sins, "and I desire to live yet a little long- "er in the world." He suffered inconceivable agony, from his wounds, and died on the fourth day.

Many a soldier has wept over his grave. He was a brave man and much beloved. He suffered twenty deaths. —I have seen the big drops chase each other down his forehead with pain and anguish. There was much sensibility and sympathy throughout the camp— I would not have, unjustly and unnecessarily, signed this death warrant for all the wealth of all the Indies. The soldiers detailed to shoot Lewis had,

from strong feelings of sympathy, or mistaken humanity failed to shoot him —but four balls had entered his body.

"An Eye Witness" appeals to Col. Russell, who he thinks now lives in Alabama, for the perfect truth of this sketch. He does not fear but the Colonel will keenly recollect and faithfully depict the horrors of the day on which six Americans were shot to death under his command—but not by his orders.

The order bears date the very day after General Jackson returned in triumph to New Orleans, and the day before he joyfully went, under triumphal arches, to the Temple of the living God; where, says the historian, "they crowned their adored General with laurels." The order for the execution of these six unhappy men bears date January 22, 1815. His crown of laurels had not yet withered, when blood, the life's blood of his countrymen, of his fellow soldiers, flowed plentifully by his order. May that order and its consequences, sink deep into the hearts of the American people and steel them against him who had no flesh in his obdurate heart; who did not feel for Man; in the midst of Joy and Revelry, almost in the more immediate presence of his Creator, he insured the fatal order to put his fellow creatures to death, and to make their wives & children, widows and orphans.

Poor JOHN WOODS

THOMAS HART BENTON

Opposite page: An
anti-Jackson poster

Above: A cartoon
showing Jackson
dismissing his
cabinet members

Right: A caricature
of Jackson from
a storybook

C.W.JEFFERYS

Chapter 6

Long Live the Union

President Jackson was a strong believer in the states' rights to determine their own laws. He did not, however, believe that the states had the right to threaten the existence of the Union. During his administration two issues arose that seriously endangered the Union. One bordered on civil war and the other on the complete collapse of the American economy.

To protect American manufacturers from the competition of cheaper imported goods, Congress placed high tariffs, or taxes, on foreign goods. As a result, foreign countries were selling fewer goods to the United States. Since they sold less, they had less money to buy cotton from the South. And since the South sold less cotton and could not buy the cheaper manufactured goods from foreigners, it was forced to buy expensive manufactured goods from the North. Without a doubt, the tariff favored Northern manufacturers.

Opposite page: Jackson toasts the Union.

Vice-President John C. Calhoun

Its economy depressed, South Carolina threatened to simply disregard the new tariff laws. Vice-President John C. Calhoun supported his home state. He published an unsigned pamphlet proposing his theory of state nullification. In it he implied that a state could nullify, or disregard, a federal law that threatened its rights. And if the federal government would not allow this, the state had the right to secede from the Union.

Outraged by the pamphlet, Jackson pleaded with the people of South Carolina to reconsider their defiance. The nation was supreme, he argued, not the states. "Disunion by armed force is treason," he said. And treason is punishable by death. Jackson further stated that within two months he could have a hundred thousand men inside South Carolina to maintain order, if necessary.

Senator Henry Clay

A week after Jackson delivered his message, South Carolina expressed a willingness to work out a compromise. John C. Calhoun resigned as vice-president to become a senator for South Carolina, hoping to work out a settlement. But it was Kentucky Senator Henry Clay who succeeded. On February 12, 1833, Clay proposed a Compromise Tariff that would reduce tariffs over a ten-year period. South Carolina finally accepted the bill, and Jackson signed the Compromise Tariff on March 2, 1833, just as his first term in office ended.

79

Above and opposite page: An anti-Adams campaign
booklet circulated by Jackson's supporters during the
1832 presidential race

When Andrew Jackson was running for a second term, there was a new method for choosing presidential candidates. No longer were candidates chosen in state legislatures or in special meetings called caucuses. For the first time, a national political convention would choose the candidates. The 1832 Democratic National Party Convention unanimously nominated Andrew Jackson for president. The National Republican Party chose Henry Clay. When the election was taken to the polls, Jackson and his running mate, Martin Van Buren, won an overwhelming victory. The chief issue of Jackson's campaign, rechartering the Second Bank of the United States, became a battleground for political war throughout his second term.

Although this bank was originally set up by private businessmen to regulate the credit and currency operations

"... Not to understand a treasure's worth,
Till time has stolen away the slighted good,
Is cause of half the poverty we feel,
And makes the world the wilderness it is.

THIS IS

THE WEALTH

that lay
In the House that Jonathan built.

Spawn'd in the muddy beds of Nile, came forth
Polluting Egypt: gardens, fields, and plains,
Were cover'd with the pest;
The croaking noisome furk'd in every nook;
No palaces, nor even chambers, scap'd;
And the land stank—so numerous was the fry."

THESE ARE

THE VERMIN

That plunder the Wealth
That lay in the House,
That Jonathan built.

"Once enslaved, farewell!
Do I forbode impossible events,
And tremble at vain dreams? Heav'n grant I may!"

THIS IS

THE THING,

That despite of attacks,
And attempts to restrain it
By villanous acts,
Will poison the vermin
That plunder the wealth,
That lay in the House
That Jonathan built.

Ay—this is the Roman,
Who acts as a King,
Who dishonours our country,
And would put down the Thing,
That despite of attacks,
And attempts to restrain it,
By villanous acts,
Will poison the Vermin,
That plunder the Wealth,
That lay in the House
That Jonathan built.

" Portentous, unexampled, unexplain'd!
What man seeing this,
And having human feelings, does not blush,
And hang his head, to think himself a man?
I cannot rest
A silent witness of the headlong rage,
Or heedless folly, by which thousands die—
Bleed gold for Ministers to sport away."

AND THESE ARE

THE PEOPLE,

All tatter'd and torn,
Who lament the sad day
When the "Hero" was born;
Who once gave him praise,

But who now give him scorn:
They lament with the victims
Of high-handed power,
Who groan in a prison
To this very hour:
Who despise the base Traitor,
To glory unknown,
Who would barter his country
And fawn at a throne.
Yes, these are the men, who with high-handed power,
Hold our clergy in prison to this very hour:
The friends of the "Roman,"
Who acts as a king,
Who despises our country,
And would put down the Thing,
That despite of attacks,
And attempts to restrain it
By villanous acts,
Will poison the Vermin
That plunder the Wealth,
That lay in the House
That Jonathan built.

THE GUILTY TRIO.
" Great skill have they in palmistry, and more
To conjure clean away the gold they touch,
Conveying worthless dross into its place;
Loud when they beg, dumb only when they steal.
Dream after dream ensues!
And still they dream, that they shall still succeed,
And still are disappointed."

AND HERE ARE

THE TRIO

Of cabinet fame,
Amos Kendall and Lewis, and Blair of bad name,
The scullions who grovel and revel in shame:
Ay—these are the tyrants—the rulers of him,
Who, enfeebled by years, is in intellect dim,
The dotard of sixty—who, "born to command,"
Dishonours himself, and would ruin the land.
Ay—these are the minions the People oppose,
Apostates, and Tories, and Liberty's foes—
The friends of the Traitor, to glory unknown,
Who would barter his country, and fawn at a throne.

Yes, these are the men, who with high-handed power,
Hold our clergy in prison to this very hour:
The friends of the "Roman,"
Who acts as a king,
Who despises our country,
And would put down the thing,
That despite of attacks,
And attempts to restrain it,
By villanous acts,
Will poison the vermin,
That plunder the Wealth,
That lay in the House
That Jonathan built.

" Burghers, men immaculate perhaps
In all their private functions, once combin'd,
Become a loathsome body, only fit
For dissolution.
Power usurp'd
Is weakness when oppos'd, conscious of wrong,
'Tis pusillanimous and prone to flight.
I could endure
Chains nowhere patiently; and chains at home,
Where I am free by birth-right, not at all."

And this is Reform—the Reform of our Yeomen—
Who have slumbered too long with a Despot in Power—
Let them rouse for the contest, and show themselves Free-
men,

November. November—the second's the hour!
Let the blood of our sires, and the spirit that warmed it,
But impart a faint glow in the breast of each son,
And "the fight of good faith" will be fought as it should be,
And the battle for Right and for Liberty won.

of the country, one-fifth of its monies came from the federal government. The national bank had enormous influence. It controlled state banks and had a monopoly on government business. Interest on federal funds that were invested in the bank went to wealthy stockholders who were splitting the profits. And since the bank was privately owned, the government could not regulate it. This alarmed Jackson the most. He saw any institution that was independent of the government and the people as a threat to American democracy.

Thus, when the national bank began granting favors to politicians and contributing money to Jackson's political opponents, Jackson vowed to destroy it. Through the brilliant use of his presidential powers, Jackson masterminded its collapse.

Patiently, Jackson waited for the rechartering of the bank to come before Congress. When Congress voted to renew its charter, Jackson vetoed it. Then he ordered the withdrawal of all government deposits from the bank. The bank tried to get even with Jackson by refusing to lend money to new businesses. But this did not work, and the bank was forced to close.

Jackson had the support of most Americans in the "bank war." They stood behind him as he closed the bank that had the "money and power to control the government and change its character." Jackson's answer to those who criticized his move was simple. He said, "The Monster was likely to destroy our republican institutions, and would have entirely subverted them if it had not been arrested in its course."

A cartoon showing Jackson and two advisers discussing the nation's surplus money

During the period of the bank war, the government sold a vast amount of land in the West, and foreign trade hit an all-time high. The surplus money coming in from tariffs and the sale of public land allowed President Jackson to pay off the national debt on January 8, 1835. For the first and last time in American history, the United States did not owe money to anyone. No other president since Jackson has been able to do this. But the government had little time to enjoy its surplus. By 1837, shortly after Jackson retired from office, financial panic swept the country.

Above: A cartoon on the fall of the bank
Below: "Funny Money" from Jackson's time
Opposite, top: Scenes of the economic crisis of 1837
Opposite, bottom: The Bank of the United States

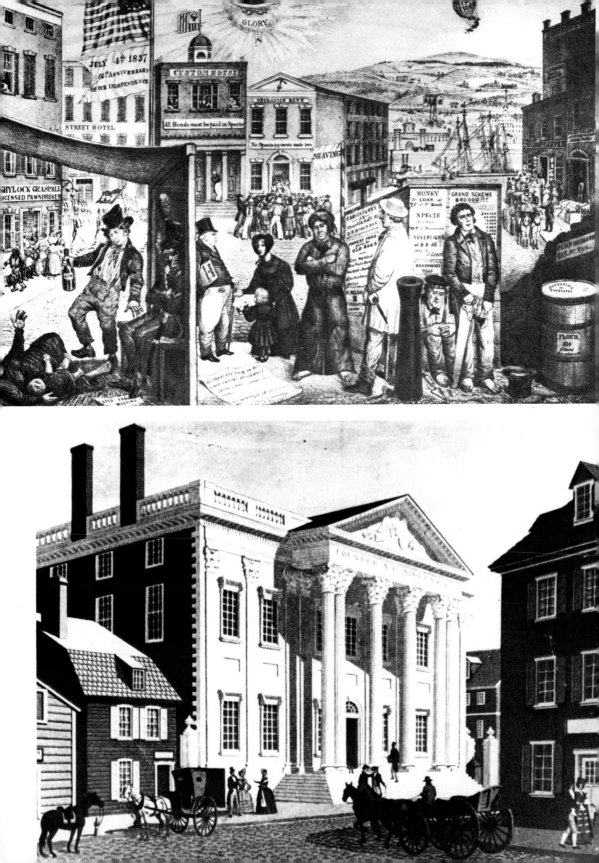

Andrew Jackson

In His Last Days.

Chapter 7

A General's Farewell

Andrew Jackson retired from office on March 4, 1837, at the age of seventy. He was confident that the office of president would be safe in the hands of Martin Van Buren, the man who had served him so well as vice-president. On inauguration day, Van Buren shared the platform with the retiring president. Although thousands of people crowded near the Capitol, it was said that they seemed "less interested in welcoming the new administration than expressing their love for the old." Eight years had passed since a similar crowd had met in Washington to cheer President Andrew Jackson, a champion of the people. The 1837 crowd was different. They were silent, perhaps with reverence for the "old, worn-out champion" who had fought their causes and had brought the country through difficult times.

Americans who stood before Jackson this time had seen him lead the country through a bank crisis and past the fears of secession. They had seen the creation of a new Democratic Party, payment of the national debt, and expansion, of America into territories that would later become the states of Arkansas, Michigan, Texas, and Florida. Many had seen reforms in education and women's rights. They had witnessed the growing opinion that slavery should be abolished. And they now marveled at exciting inventions that were changing their lives: the horse-drawn streetcar, steam locomotive, McCormick reaper, and an early form of baseball. Eight years had made a difference. This was a new time, an age of experimentation and change. And Andrew seemed to symbolize it all.

His farewell speech to the American people was affectionate, though filled with concern. Cautioning the country to preserve the Union at all costs, he warned of the bitterness he saw developing between the North and the South over issues of tariffs and slavery. Touching the hearts of the people who had come to pay their final tribute to him, his closing remarks were eloquent: "I thank God that my life has been spent in a land of liberty and that he has given me a heart to love my country with the affection of a son. And filled with gratitude for your constant and unwavering kindness, I bid you a last and affectionate farewell."

After Jackson left Washington, it took him several weeks to reach the Hermitage. He visited with friends along the way and stopped for cheering crowds who followed him wherever he went. Age and ill health also

Andrew Jackson's funeral procession

slowed him down. Old wounds caused him constant pain, and he suffered from tuberculosis and dropsy. But he overcame these ills as he had overcome others before.

Life at the Hermitage was active. Jackson's daily routine included riding his horses and overseeing his cotton fields. Each day he met with office-seekers who came to ask for political favors and special assistance. Almost to the day of his death, he continued to write his views on current political affairs to loyal friends and even to the new president. When he died quietly on June 8, 1845, at the age of seventy-eight, part of an era died too. The popular frontier hero and president was gone. But the nation was strong with a new spirit of democracy that Andrew Jackson's presidency had begun.

Chronology of American History

(Shaded area covers events in Andrew Jackson's lifetime.)

About A.D. 982—Eric the Red, born in Norway, reaches Greenland in one of the first European voyages to North America.

About 985—Eric the Red brings settlers from Iceland to Greenland.

About 1000—Leif Ericson (Eric the Red's son) leads what is thought to be the first European expedition to mainland North America; Leif probably lands in Canada.

1492—Christopher Columbus, hoping to find a sea route from Spain to the Far East, discovers the New World.

1497—John Cabot reaches Canada in the first English voyage to North America.

1513—Ponce de Léon explores Florida in search of the fabled Fountain of Youth.

1519-1521—Hernando Cortés of Spain conquers Mexico.

1534—French explorers led by Jacques Cartier enter the Gulf of St. Lawrence in Canada.

1540—Spanish explorer Francisco Coronado begins exploring the American Southwest, seeking the riches of the mythical Seven Cities of Cibola.

1565—St. Augustine, Florida, the first permanent European town in what is now the United States, is founded by the Spanish.

1607—Jamestown, Virginia, is founded, the first permanent English town in the present-day U.S.

1608—Frenchman Samuel de Champlain founds the village of Quebec, Canada.

1609—Henry Hudson explores the eastern coast of present-day U.S. for the Netherlands; the Dutch then claim parts of New York, New Jersey, Delaware, and Connecticut and name the area New Netherland.

1619—The English colonies' first shipment of black slaves arrives in Jamestown.

1620—English Pilgrims found Massachusetts' first permanent town at Plymouth.

1621—Massachusetts Pilgrims and Indians hold the famous first Thanksgiving feast in colonial America.

1623—Colonization of New Hampshire is begun by the English.

1624—Colonization of present-day New York State is begun by the Dutch at Fort Orange (Albany).

1625—The Dutch start building New Amsterdam (now New York City).

1630—The town of Boston, Massachusetts, is founded by the English Puritans.

1633—Colonization of Connecticut is begun by the English.

1634—Colonization of Maryland is begun by the English.

1636—Harvard, the colonies' first college, is founded in Massachusetts. Rhode Island colonization begins when Englishman Roger Williams founds Providence.

1638—Delaware colonization begins when Swedish people build Fort Christina at present-day Wilmington.

1640—Stephen Daye of Cambridge, Massachusetts prints *The Bay Psalm Book*, the first English-language book published in what is now the U.S.

1643—Swedish settlers begin colonizing Pennsylvania.

About 1650—North Carolina is colonized by Virginia settlers.

1660—New Jersey colonization is begun by the Dutch at present-day Jersey City.

1670—South Carolina colonization is begun by the English near Charleston.

1673—Jacques Marquette and Louis Jolliet explore the upper Mississippi River for France.

1682—Philadelphia, Pennsylvania, is settled. La Salle explores Mississippi River all the way to its mouth in Louisiana and claims the whole Mississippi Valley for France.

1693—College of William and Mary is founded in Williamsburg, Virginia.

1700—Colonial population is about 250,000.

1703—Benjamin Franklin is born in Boston.

1732—George Washington, first president of the U.S., is born in Westmoreland County, Virginia.

1733—James Oglethorpe founds Savannah, Georgia; Georgia is established as the thirteenth colony.

1735—John Adams, second president of the U.S., is born in Braintree, Massachusetts.

1737—William Byrd founds Richmond, Virginia.

1738—British troops are sent to Georgia over border dispute with Spain.

1739—Black insurrection takes place in South Carolina.

1740—English Parliament passes act allowing naturalization of immigrants to American colonies after seven-year residence.

1743—Thomas Jefferson, third president of the U.S., is born in Albemarle County, Virginia. Benjamin Franklin retires at age thirty-seven to devote himself to scientific inquiries and public service.

1744—King George's War begins; France joins war effort against England.

1745—During King George's War, France raids settlements in Maine and New York.

1747—Classes begin at Princeton College in New Jersey.

1748—The Treaty of Aix-la-Chapelle concludes King George's War.

1749—Parliament legally recognizes slavery in colonies and the inauguration of the plantation system in the South. George Washington becomes the surveyor for Culpepper County in Virginia.

1750—Thomas Walker passes through and names Cumberland Gap on his way toward Kentucky region. Colonial population is about 1,200,000.

1751—James Monroe, fourth president of the U.S., is born in Port Conway, Virginia. English Parliament passes Currency Act, banning New England colonies from issuing paper money. George Washington travels to Barbados.

1752—Pennsylvania Hospital, the first general hospital in the colonies, is founded in Philadelphia. Benjamin Franklin uses a kite in a thunderstorm to demonstrate that lightning is a form of electricity.

1753—George Washington delivers command from Virginia Lieutenant Governor Dinwiddie that the French withdraw from the Ohio River Valley; French disregard the demand. Colonial population is about 1,328,000.

1754—French and Indian War begins (extends to Europe as the Seven Years' War). Washington surrenders at Fort Necessity.

1755—French and Indians ambush General Braddock. Washington becomes commander of Virginia troops.

1756—England declares war on France.

1758—James Monroe, fifth president of the U.S., is born in Westmoreland County, Virginia.

1759—Cherokee Indian war begins in southern colonies; hostilities extend to 1761. George Washington marries Martha Dandridge Custis.

1760—George III becomes king of England. Colonial population is about 1,600,000.

1762—England declares war on Spain.

1763—Treaty of Paris concludes the French and Indian War and the Seven Years' War. England gains Canada and most other French lands east of the Mississippi River.

1764—British pass the Sugar Act to gain tax money from the colonists. The issue of taxation without representation is first introduced in Boston. John Adams marries Abigail Smith.

1765—Stamp Act goes into effect in the colonies. Business virtually stops as almost all colonists refuse to use the stamps.

1766—British repeal the Stamp Act.

1767—John Quincy Adams, sixth president of the U.S. and son of second president John Adams, is born in Braintree, Massachusetts. Andrew Jackson, seventh president of the U.S., is born in Waxhaw settlement, South Carolina.

1769—Daniel Boone sights the Kentucky Territory.

1770—In the Boston Massacre, British soldiers kill five colonists and injure six. Townshend Acts are repealed, thus eliminating all duties on imports to the colonies except tea.

1771—Benjamin Franklin begins his autobiography, a work that he will never complete. The North Carolina assembly passes the "Bloody Act," which makes rioters guilty of treason.

1772—Samuel Adams rouses colonists to consider British threats to self-government. Thomas Jefferson marries Martha Wayles Skelton.

1773—English Parliament passes the Tea Act. Colonists dressed as Mohawk Indians board British tea ships and toss 342 casks of tea into the water in what becomes known as the Boston Tea Party.

1774—British close the port of Boston to punish the city for the Boston Tea Party. First Continental Congress convenes in Philadelphia.

1775—American Revolution begins with battles of Lexington and Concord, Massachusetts. Second Continental Congress opens in Philadelphia. George Washington becomes commander-in-chief of the Continental army.

1776—Declaration of Independence is adopted on July 4.

1777—Congress adopts the American flag with thirteen stars and thirteen stripes. John Adams is sent to France to negotiate peace treaty.

1778—France declares war against Great Britain and becomes U.S. ally.

1779—British surrender to Americans at Vincennes. Thomas Jefferson is elected governor of Virginia. James Madison is elected to the Continental Congress.

1780—Benedict Arnold, first American traitor, defects to the British.

1781—Articles of Confederation go into effect. Cornwallis surrenders to George Washington at Yorktown, ending the American Revolution.

1782—American commissioners, including John Adams, sign peace treaty with British in Paris. Thomas Jefferson's wife, Martha, dies.

1785—Congress adopts the dollar as the unit of currency. John Adams is made minister to Great Britain. Thomas Jefferson is appointed minister to France.

1786—Shays' Rebellion begins in Massachusetts.

1787—Constitutional Convention assembles in Philadelphia, with George Washington presiding; U.S. Constitution is adopted. Delaware, New Jersey, and Pennsylvania become states.

1788—Virginia, South Carolina, New York, Connecticut, New Hampshire, Maryland, and Massachusetts become states. U.S. Constitution is ratified. New York City is declared temporary U.S. capital.

1789—Presidential electors elect George Washington and John Adams as first president and vice-president. Thomas Jefferson is appointed secretary of state. North Carolina becomes a state. French Revolution begins.

1790—Supreme Court meets for the first time. Rhode Island becomes a state. First national census in the U.S. counts 3,929,214 persons.

1791—Vermont enters the Union. U.S. Bill of Rights, the first ten amendments to the Constitution, goes into effect. District of Columbia is established.

1792—Thomas Paine publishes *The Rights of Man*. Kentucky becomes a state. Two political parties are formed in the U.S., Federalist and Republican. Washington is elected to a second term, with Adams as vice-president.

1793—War between France and Britain begins; U.S. declares neutrality. Eli Whitney invents the cotton gin; cotton production and slave labor increase in the South.

1794—Eleventh Amendment to the Constitution is passed, limiting federal courts' power. "Whiskey Rebellion" in Pennsylvania protests federal whiskey tax. James Madison marries Dolley Payne Todd.

1795—George Washington signs the Jay Treaty with Great Britain. Treaty of San Lorenzo, between U.S. and Spain, settles Florida boundary and gives U.S. right to navigate the Mississippi.

1796—Tennessee enters the Union. Washington gives his Farewell Address, refusing a third presidential term. John Adams is elected president and Thomas Jefferson vice-president.

1797—Adams recommends defense measures against possible war with France. Napoleon Bonaparte and his army march against Austrians in Italy. U.S. population is about 4,900,000.

1798—Washington is named commander-in-chief of the U.S. army. Department of the Navy is created. Alien and Sedition Acts are passed. Napoleon's troops invade Egypt and Switzerland.

1799—George Washington dies at Mount Vernon. James Monroe is elected governor of Virginia. French Revolution ends. Napoleon becomes ruler of France.

1800—Thomas Jefferson and Aaron Burr tie for president. U.S. capital is moved from Philadelphia to Washington, D.C. The White House is built as presidents' home. Spain returns Louisiana to France.

1801—After thirty-six ballots, House of Representatives elects Thomas Jefferson president, making Burr vice-president. James Madison is named secretary of state.

1802—Congress abolishes excise taxes. U.S. Military Academy is founded at West Point, New York.

1803—Ohio enters the Union. Louisiana Purchase treaty is signed with France, greatly expanding U.S. territory.

1804—Twelfth Amendment to the Constitution rules that president and vice-president be elected separately. Alexander Hamilton is killed by Vice-President Aaron Burr in a duel. Orleans Territory is established. Napoleon crowns himself emperor of France.

1805—Thomas Jefferson begins his second term as president. Lewis and Clark expedition reaches the Pacific Ocean.

1806—Coinage of silver dollars is stopped; resumes in 1836.

1807—Aaron Burr is acquitted in treason trial. Embargo Act closes U.S. ports to trade.

1808—James Madison is elected president. Congress outlaws importing slaves from Africa.

1810—U.S. population is 7,240,000.

1811—General William Henry Harrison defeats Indians at Tippecanoe. James Monroe is named secretary of state.

1812—Louisiana becomes a state. U.S. declares war on Britain (War of 1812). James Madison is reelected president. Napoleon invades Russia.

1813—British forces take Fort Niagara and Buffalo, New York.

1814—Francis Scott Key writes "The Star-Spangled Banner." British troops burn much of Washington, D.C., including the White House. Treaty of Ghent ends War of 1812. James Monroe becomes secretary of war.

1815 — Napoleon meets his final defeat at Battle of Waterloo.

1816 — James Monroe is elected president. Indiana becomes a state.

1817 — Mississippi becomes a state. Construction on Erie Canal begins.

1818 — Illinois enters the Union. The present thirteen-stripe flag is adopted. Border between U.S. and Canada is agreed upon.

1819 — Alabama becomes a state. U.S. purchases Florida from Spain. Thomas Jefferson establishes the University of Virginia.

1820 — James Monroe is reelected. In the Missouri Compromise, Maine enters the Union as a free (non-slave) state.

1821 — Missouri enters the Union as a slave state. Santa Fe Trail opens the American Southwest. Mexico declares independence from Spain. Napoleon Bonaparte dies.

1822 — U.S. recognizes Mexico and Colombia. Liberia in Africa is founded as a home for freed slaves.

1823 — Monroe Doctrine closes North and South America to colonizing or invasion by European powers.

1824 — House of Representatives elects John Quincy Adams president when none of the four candidates wins a majority in national election. Mexico becomes a republic.

1825 — Erie Canal is opened. U.S. population is 11,300,000.

1826 — Thomas Jefferson and John Adams both die on July 4, the fiftieth anniversary of the Declaration of Independence.

1828 — Andrew Jackson is elected president. Tariff of Abominations is passed by Congress, cutting imports.

1829 — James Madison attends Virginia's constitutional convention. Slavery is abolished in Mexico.

1830 — Indian Removal Act to resettle Indians west of the Mississippi is approved.

1831 — James Monroe dies in New York City. Cyrus McCormick develops his reaper.

1832 — Andrew Jackson, nominated by the new Democratic Party, is reelected president.

1833 — Britain abolishes slavery in its colonies.

1835 — Federal government becomes debt-free for the first time.

1836 — Martin Van Buren becomes president. Texas wins independence from Mexico. Arkansas joins the Union. James Madison dies at Montpelier, Virginia.

1837 — Michigan enters the Union. U.S. population is 15,900,000.

1840 — William Henry Harrison is elected president.

1841 — President Harrison dies one month after inauguration. Vice-President John Tyler succeeds him.

1844 — James Knox Polk is elected president. Samuel Morse sends first telegraphic message.

1845 — Texas and Florida become states. Potato famine in Ireland causes massive emigration from Ireland to U.S. Andrew Jackson dies near Nashville, Tennessee.

1846 — Iowa enters the Union. War with Mexico begins.

1847 — U.S. captures Mexico City.

1848 — Zachary Taylor becomes president. Treaty of Guadalupe Hidalgo ends Mexico-U.S. war. Wisconsin becomes a state.

1850 — President Taylor dies and Vice-President Millard Fillmore succeeds him. California enters the Union, breaking tie between slave and free states.

1852 — Franklin Pierce is elected president.

1853 — Gadsen Purchase transfers Mexican territory to U.S.

1854 — "War for Bleeding Kansas" is fought between slave and free states.

1855 — Czar Nicholas I of Russia dies, succeeded by Alexander II.

1856 — James Buchanan is elected president. In Massacre of Potawatomi Creek, Kansas-slavers are murdered by free-staters.

1858 — Minnesota enters the Union.

1859 — Oregon becomes a state.

1860 — Abraham Lincoln is elected president; South Carolina secedes from the Union in protest.

1861 — Arkansas, Tennessee, North Carolina, and Virginia secede. Kansas enters the Union as a free state. Civil War begins.

1862 — Union forces capture Fort Henry, Roanoke Island, Fort Donelson, Jacksonville, and New Orleans; Union armies are defeated at the battles of Bull Run and Fredericksburg.

1863 — Lincoln issues Emancipation Proclamation: all slaves held in rebelling territories are declared free. West Virginia becomes a state.

1864 — Abraham Lincoln is reelected. Nevada becomes a state.

1865 — Lincoln is assassinated, succeeded by Andrew Johnson. U.S. Civil War ends on May 26. Thirteenth Amendment abolishes slavery.

1867 — Nebraska becomes a state. U.S. buys Alaska from Russia for $7,200,000. Reconstruction Acts are passed.

1868 — President Johnson is impeached for violating Tenure of Office Act, but is acquitted by Senate. Ulysses S. Grant is elected president. Fourteenth Amendment prohibits voting discrimination.

1870 — Fifteenth Amendment gives blacks the right to vote.

1872 — Grant is reelected over Horace Greeley. General Amnesty Act pardons ex-Confederates.

1876 — Colorado enters the Union. "Custer's last stand": he and his men are massacred by Sioux Indians at Little Big Horn, Montana.

1877 — Rutherford B. Hayes is elected president as all disputed votes are awarded to him.

1880 — James A. Garfield is elected president.

1881 — President Garfield is shot and killed, succeeded by Vice-President Chester A. Arthur.

1882 — U.S. bans Chinese immigration for ten years.

1884 — Grover Cleveland becomes president.

1886 — Statue of Liberty is dedicated.

1888 — Benjamin Harrison is elected president.

1889 — North Dakota, South Dakota, Washington, and Montana become states.

1890 — Idaho and Wyoming become states.

1892 — Grover Cleveland is elected president.

1896 — William McKinley is elected president. Utah becomes a state.

1898 — U.S. declares war on Spain over Cuba.

1899 — Philippines demand independence from U.S.

1900 — McKinley is reelected. Boxer Rebellion against foreigners in China begins.

1901 — McKinley is assassinated by anarchist; he is succeeded by Theodore Roosevelt.

1902 — U.S. acquires perpetual control over Panama Canal.

1903 — Alaskan frontier is settled.

1904 — Russian-Japanese War breaks out. Theodore Roosevelt wins presidential election.

1905 — Treaty of Portsmouth signed, ending Russian-Japanese War.

1906 — U.S. troops occupy Cuba.

1907 — President Roosevelt bars all Japanese immigration. Oklahoma enters the Union.

1908 — William Howard Taft becomes president.

1909 — NAACP is founded under W.E.B. DuBois

1910 — China abolishes slavery.

1911 — Chinese Revolution begins.

1912 — Woodrow Wilson is elected president. Arizona and New Mexico become states.

1913 — Federal income tax is introduced in U.S. through the Sixteenth Amendment.

1914 — World War I begins.

1915 — British liner *Lusitania* is sunk by German submarine.

1916 — Wilson is reelected president.

1917 — U.S. breaks diplomatic relations with Germany. Czar Nicholas of Russia abdicates as revolution begins. U.S. declares war on Austria-Hungary.

1918 — Wilson proclaims "Fourteen Points" as war aims. On November 11, armistice is signed between Allies and Germany.

1919 — Eighteenth Amendment prohibits sale and manufacture of intoxicating liquors. Wilson presides over first League of Nations; wins Nobel Peace Prize.

1920 — Nineteenth Amendment (women's suffrage) is passed. Warren Harding is elected president.

1921 — Adolf Hitler's stormtroopers begin to terrorize political opponents.

1922 — Irish Free State is established. Soviet states form USSR. Benito Mussolini forms Fascist government in Italy.

1923 — President Harding dies; he is succeeded by Vice-President Calvin Coolidge.

1924 — Coolidge is elected president.

1925 — Hitler reorganizes Nazi Party and publishes first volume of *Mein Kampf.*

1926 — Fascist youth organizations founded in Germany and Italy. Republic of Lebanon proclaimed.

1927 — Stalin becomes Soviet dictator. Economic conference in Geneva attended by fifty-two nations.

1928 — Herbert Hoover is elected president. U.S. and many other nations sign Kellogg-Briand pacts to outlaw war.

1929 — Stock prices in New York crash on "Black Thursday"; the Great Depression begins.

1930 — Bank of U.S. and its many branches close (most significant bank failure of the year).

1931 — Emigration from U.S. exceeds immigration for first time as Depression deepens.

1932 — Franklin D. Roosevelt wins presidential election in a Democratic landslide.

1933 — First concentration camps are erected in Germany. U.S. recognizes USSR and resumes trade. Twenty-First Amendment repeals prohibition.

1934 — Severe dust storms hit Plains states. President Roosevelt passes U.S. Social Security Act.

1936 — Roosevelt is reelected. Spanish Civil War begins. Hitler and Mussolini form Rome-Berlin Axis.

1937 — Roosevelt signs Neutrality Act.

1938 — Roosevelt sends appeal to Hitler and Mussolini to settle European problems amicably.

1939 — Germany takes over Czechoslovakia and invades Poland, starting World War II.

1940—Roosevelt is reelected for a third term.

1941—Japan bombs Pearl Harbor, U.S. declares war on Japan. Germany and Italy declare war on U.S.; U.S. then declares war on them.

1942—Allies agree not to make separate peace treaties with the enemies. U.S. government transfers more than 100,000 Nisei (Japanese-Americans) from west coast to inland concentration camps.

1943—Allied bombings of Germany begin.

1944—Roosevelt is reelected for a fourth term. Allied forces invade Normandy on D-Day.

1945—President Roosevelt dies; he is succeeded by Harry S Truman. Mussolini is killed; Hitler commits suicide. Germany surrenders. U.S. drops atomic bomb on Hiroshima; Japan surrenders: end of World War II.

1946—U.N. General Assembly holds its first session in London. Peace conference of twenty-one nations is held in Paris.

1947—Peace treaties are signed in Paris. "Cold War" is in full swing.

1948—U.S. passes Marshall Plan Act, providing $17 billion in aid for Europe. U.S. recognizes new nation of Israel. India and Pakistan become free of British rule. Truman is elected president.

1949—Republic of Eire is proclaimed in Dublin. Russia blocks land route access from Western Germany to Berlin; airlift begins. U.S., France, and Britain agree to merge their zones of occupation in West Germany. Apartheid program begins in South Africa.

1950—Riots in Johannesburg, South Africa, against apartheid. North Korea invades South Korea. U.N. forces land in South Korea and recapture Seoul.

1951—Twenty-Second Amendment limits president to two terms.

1952—Dwight D. Eisenhower resigns as supreme commander in Europe and is elected president.

1953—Stalin dies; struggle for power in Russia follows. The Rosenbergs, first sentenced as spies in 1951, are executed.

1954—U.S. and Japan sign mutual defense agreement.

1955—Blacks in Montgomery, Alabama, boycott segregated bus lines.

1956—Eisenhower is reelected president. Soviet troops march into Hungary.

1957—U.S. agrees to withdraw ground forces from Japan. Russia launches first satellite, *Sputnik*.

1958—European Common Market comes into being. Alaska becomes the forty-ninth state. Fidel Castro begins war against Batista government in Cuba.

1959—Hawaii becomes fiftieth state. Castro becomes premier of Cuba. De Gaulle is proclaimed president of the Fifth Republic of France.

1960—Historic debates between Senator John F. Kennedy and Vice-President Richard Nixon are televised. Kennedy is elected president. Brezhnev becomes president of USSR.

1961—Berlin Wall is constructed. Kennedy and Khrushchev confer in Vienna. In Bay of Pigs incident, Cubans trained by CIA attempt to overthrow Castro.

1962—U.S. military council is established in South Vietnam.

1963—Riots and beatings by police and whites mark civil rights demonstrations in Birmingham, Alabama; 30,000 troops are called out, Martin Luther King, Jr., is arrested. Freedom marchers descend on Washington, D.C., to demonstrate. President Kennedy is assassinated; Vice-President Lyndon B. Johnson is sworn in as president.

1964—U.S. aircraft bomb North Vietnam. Johnson is elected president.

1965—U.S. combat troops arrive in South Vietnam.

1966—International Days of Protest against U.S. policy in Vietnam. National Guard quells race riots in Chicago.

1967—Six-Day War between Israel and Arab nations.

1968—Martin Luther King, Jr., is assassinated in Memphis, Tennessee. Senator Robert Kennedy is assassinated in Los Angeles. Riots and police brutality take place at Democratic National Convention in Chicago. Richard Nixon is elected president. Czechoslovakia is invaded by Soviet and Warsaw Pact troops.

1969—Hundreds of thousands of people in several U.S. cities demonstrate against Vietnam War.

1970—Four Vietnam War protesters are killed by National Guardsmen at Kent State University in Ohio.

1971—Twenty-Sixth Amendment allows eighteen-year-olds to vote.

1972—Nixon visits Communist China; is reelected president in near-record landslide. Watergate affair begins when five men are arrested in the Watergate hotel complex in Washington, D.C. Nixon announces resignations of aides Haldeman, Ehrlichman, and Dean and Attorney General Kleindienst as a result of Watergate-related charges.

1973—Vice-President Spiro Agnew resigns; Gerald Ford is named vice-president. Vietnam peace treaty is formally approved after nineteen months of negotiations.

1974—As a result of Watergate cover-up, impeachment is considered; Nixon resigns and Ford becomes president. Ford pardons Nixon and grants limited amnesty to Vietnam War draft evaders and military deserters.

1975—U.S. civilians are evacuated from Saigon, South Vietnam, as Communist forces complete takeover of South Vietnam.

1976—U.S. celebrates its Bicentennial. James Earl Carter becomes president.

1977—Carter pardons most Vietnam draft evaders, numbering some 10,000.

1980—Ronald Reagan is elected president.

1981—President Reagan is shot in the chest in assassination attempt. Sandra Day O'Connor is appointed first woman justice of the Supreme Court.

1983—U.S. troops invade island of Grenada.

1984—Reagan is reelected president. Democratic candidate Walter Mondale's running mate, Geraldine Ferraro, is the first woman selected for vice-president by a major U.S. political party.

1985—Soviet Communist Party secretary Konstantin Chernenko dies; Mikhail Gorbachev succeeds him. U.S. and Soviet officials discuss arms control in Geneva. Reagan and Gorbachev hold summit conference in Geneva. Racial tensions accelerate in South Africa.

1986—Space shuttle *Challenger* crashes shortly after takeoff; crew of seven dies. U.S. bombs bases in Libya. Corazon Aquino defeats Ferdinand Marcos in Philippine presidential election.

Index

Page numbers in boldface type indicate illustrations.

About the Author

    Alice Osinski is a Chicago-based free-lance writer and photo researcher. She holds a B.A. in Social Sciences with special coursework in American Indian Studies. After teaching American Indian children for seven years in Pine Ridge, South Dakota, and Gallup, New Mexico, Ms. Osinski launched her career in writing. She has developed bicultural curricula for alternative school programs in South Dakota and New Mexico. Several of her articles and children's stories appear in textbooks for D.C. Heath and Open Court. Other books she has written for Childrens Press include *The Sioux*, *The Navajo*, *The Chippewa*, and *The Eskimo*.

DATE DUE
